T5-AOM-614

3495 North Victoria
Shoreview, MN 55126

**Donated
To The Library by**

THE PATTY DULING
FAMILY

© DEMCO, INC. 1990
PRINTED IN U.S.A.

Inside the NFL

THE PHILADELPHIA EAGLES

St. Odilia School Library
3495 North Victoria
Shoreview, MN 55126

BOB ITALIA
ABDO & Daughters

Published by Abdo & Daughters, 4940 Viking Drive, Suite 622, Edina, Minnesota 55435.

Copyright © 1996 by Abdo Consulting Group, Inc., Pentagon Tower, P.O. Box 36036, Minneapolis, Minnesota 55435 USA. International copyrights reserved in all countries. No part of this book may be reproduced in any form without written permission from the publisher.

Printed in the United States.

Cover Photo credits: Wide World Photos/Allport Photos
Interior Photo credits: Wide World Photos, pages 5, 7, 13, 18, 19, 21, 24, 25
      Bettmann Photos, pages 4, 6, 8, 10, 18, 19, 23
      Allsport, page 22

Edited by Kal Gronvall

Library of Congress Cataloging-in-Publication Data

Italia, Bob, 1955-
The Philadelphia Eagles / Bob Italia.
  p. cm. -- (Inside the NFL)
Includes index.
Summary: Traces the history of this football team since 1933 and Includes contributions of star players such as Reggie White, Randall Cunningham, and Ron Jaworski.
  ISBN 1-56239-528-9
1. Philadelphia Eagles (Football team)--History--Juvenile literature. [1. Philadelphia Eagles (Football team)--History. 2. Football--History.] I. Title. II. Series: Italia, Bob, 1955- Inside the NFL.
GV956.P44I83 1995
796.332'64'0374811--dc20   95-30559
                           CIP
                           AC

CONTENTS

Star Players, Few Titles 4
From Yellow Jackets to Eagles 6
Van Buren 7
Bednarik 9
NFL Champions 10
Vermeil 12
"Jaws" 13
A Super Season 16
The Minister of Defense 20
Randall 22
Division Champs 24
Surprise Starts 27
Glossary 29
Index 31

Star Players, Few Titles

The Philadelphia Eagles have had many of the National Football League's (NFL's) great players. Linebacker Chuck Bednarik, and quarterbacks Norm Van Brocklin and Sonny Jurgenson all wore Eagles' jerseys. Yet the Eagles last NFL championship win was in 1960. They have yet to win a Super Bowl Championship.

In 1980, the Eagles assembled another championship-quality team. They had quarterback Ron Jaworski, defensive end Reggie White, running back Wilbert Montgomery, and tight end Harold Carmichael. But they failed to capture the title against the Oakland Raiders.

The addition of defensive linemen Jerome Brown and Clyde Simmons, and quarterback Randall Cunningham made the Eagles mighty once again in the late 1980s.

Philadelphia often led the NFL in defense. Cunningham's passing and running ability made him one of the most feared quarterbacks in the league. But despite all their talent, these Eagles could never soar to the top of the NFL.

Cunningham remains with the team. But White and Brown are gone. Having lost many of their star players, the Eagles face a period of slowly rebuilding their once mighty defense. Until that time, Eagles fans can relish the long passes and mad scrambling of their lanky star quarterback.

Norm Van Brocklin helped turn the Eagles into winners.

Randall Cunningham's passing and running ability made him one of the most feared quarterbacks in the league.

From Yellow Jackets to Eagles

In 1933, the Philadelphia Eagles—formerly known as the Frankfort Yellow Jackets— played their first season in the National Football League (NFL). Bert Bell and college friend Lud Wray bought the team for $2,800 and moved it to Philadelphia.

Quarterback Davey O'Brien being rushed by the defense when playing college ball for the Texas Christian team.

Bell wanted the Eagles to be the NFL's best team. But from 1933 to 1942, Philadelphia suffered 10 straight losing seasons. Bell got so frustrated, he even acted as head coach. But even he could not help the team.

In the late 1930s, the Eagles improved slightly when quarterback Davey O'Brien led the offense. But Philadelphia never finished higher than fourth in the five-team Eastern Division. Finally, Bell had had enough. He sold the team in 1941.

Alexis Thompson, a wealthy steel executive from New York, bought the Eagles. Thompson then hired Earl "Greasy" Neale as head coach. Neale proved to be a good coach. But he needed more talent with which to work. In 1944, he finally got a player who could turn the team's fortunes around.

Van Buren

To improve the offense, the Eagles drafted Steve Van Buren in 1944. Van Buren was an outstanding running back from Louisiana State University. Quarterback Tommy Thompson, fullback Pete Pihos, and Van Buren gave the Eagles one of the best offenses in the league.

From 1947 to 1949, Philadelphia captured the Eastern Division three straight years. The Eagles also won the league championship in 1948 and 1949. By then, Van Buren had become one of the league's top rushers, and Thompson was the best passer in the NFL.

After the 1949 championship, the Eagles returned to mediocrity. Throughout most of the 1950s, the Eagles never challenged for the division title. Van Buren eventually retired. But a new defensive star was emerging—a star who was born and raised in Philadelphia. His name was Chuck Bednarik.

Steve Van Buren, running back for the Philadelphia Eagles.

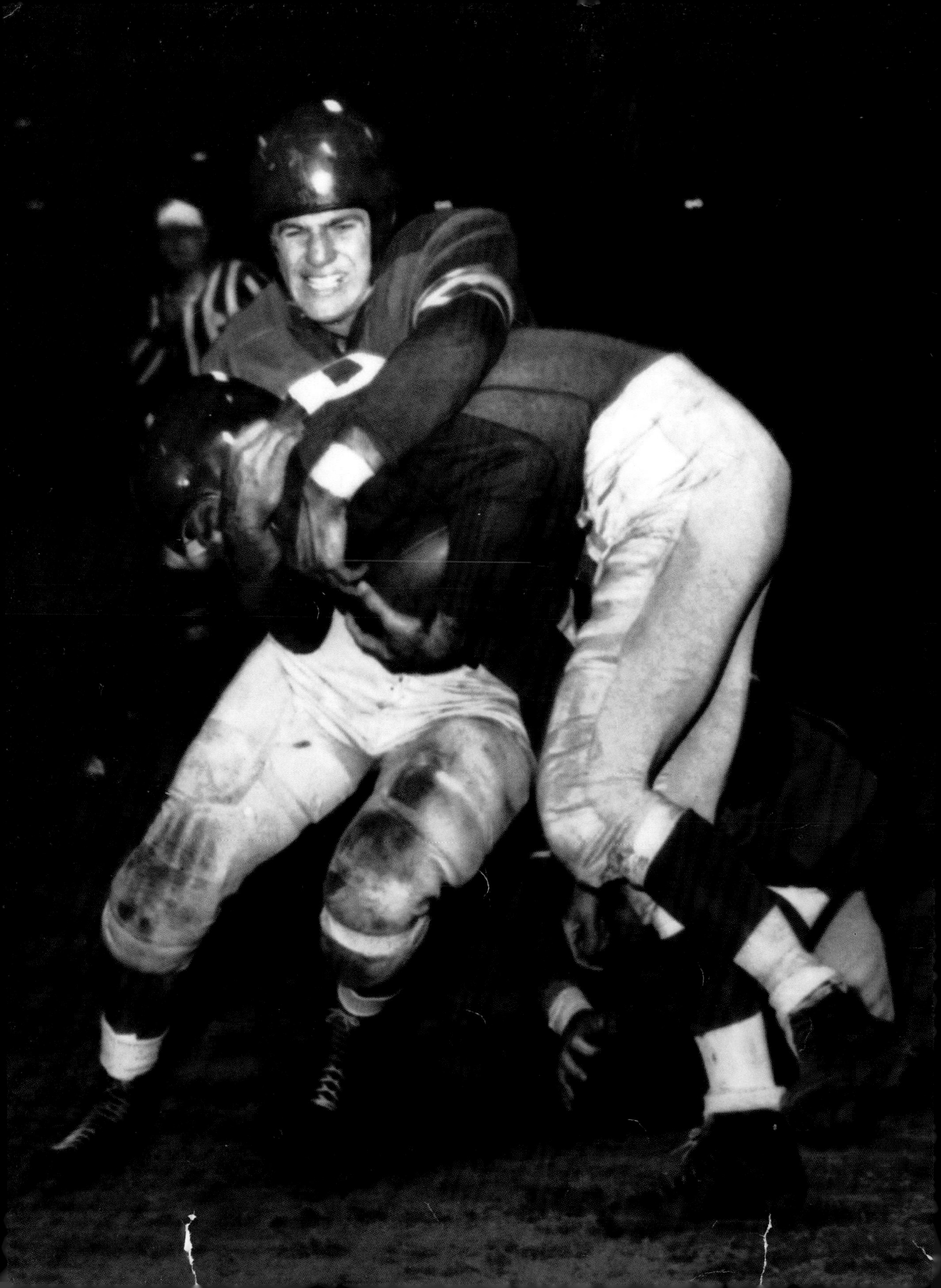

Bednarik

Chuck Bednarik was a tough football player. Though often injured, he played with reckless abandon. Throughout his career, Bednarik had broken bones, torn tendons, and separated shoulders. But they never seemed to bother him.

Bednarik signed with the Eagles in 1949 and immediately became the starting linebacker. Eventually, he became known as the "60-Minute Man" because he also played center and rarely left the game. During his 12-year career, Bednarik earned All-Pro honors 8 times.

In 1958, Bednarik's 60-minute games ended when he suffered a knee injury that prevented him from playing linebacker. But he remained the Eagles' center, and snapped the ball to Philadelphia's new star player—quarterback Norm Van Brocklin.

Van Brocklin came to the Eagles in a trade with the Los Angeles Rams. Philadelphia had to give the Rams a first-round draft choice and two starters to get Van Brocklin. But Philadelphia got the better of the trade. Van Brocklin was a smart and talented leader. He eventually turned the Eagles into champions once again.

In 1960, Van Brocklin led the Eagles to a division title. Throughout the season, the team often fell behind—only to rally in the second half. The Eagles trailed at halftime in 5 games, sometimes by 24 points. But each time at halftime, Van Brocklin went to the blackboard and explained to his teammates what the opposing defense was doing. With these insights, Philadelphia often came back to win in the second half.

**Opposite page:
Eagle linebacker Chuck Bednarik
tackles the Giants quarterback in 1949.**

NFL Champions

As the season progressed, injuries began hurting the team. Two linebackers were lost for the season, and coach Buck Shaw did not want to bring new players onto the team. Instead, he turned to an old warrior: Chuck Bednarik. Bednarik thought his linebacking days were over. But the Eagles needed his experience to get them to the championship game.

For one last time in his career, Bednarik played center and linebacker for the rest of the season. Teamed with cornerback Tom Brookshier, Bednarik led the defense as the Eagles won the Eastern Division title. For the first time in 11 years, Philadelphia would play for the NFL championship.

The Eagles played the Green Bay Packers at Philadelphia's Franklin Field. The game looked like a mismatch. The Packers had many talented players, including quarterback Bart Starr, and legendary head coach Vince Lombardi. The Packers were also a young and strong team, with many players in their mid-twenties.

The Eagles, however, were getting old and losing their fire. Their head coach, starting quarterback, and center/linebacker were playing their last game with the team. During the season, Shaw had announced he would retire once the season ended. Van Brocklin would not return to the Eagles in 1961, and Bednarik would finally call it quits after an impressive 12-year career. But first, they had a championship to win. In Bednarik's mind, there was no better way to say good-bye to the game he loved so much. Bednarik also knew that to win that championship, he would have to play on offense and defense one more time.

Once the game began, the Packers had trouble with the Philadelphia defense. The Eagles did not do anything fancy. They just swarmed all over their opponent.

As time ticked away in the fourth quarter, the Eagles held on to a 17-13 lead. But then Starr took the Packers on one last drive into Philadelphia territory.

On the game's final play, Starr threw a pass to fullback Jim Taylor. Taylor streaked down the right sideline and then cut into the middle. He was only 10 yards away from the endzone and looked like he was about to score. But Bednarik was not going to let that happen. Out of nowhere, Bednarik tackled Taylor and fell on top of him as the last few seconds ticked away.

Bednarik could see the clock at one corner of Franklin Field. Taylor squirming and shouted at Bednarik to move. But Bednarik did not budge until the clock hit the zero mark. "OK, Jimmy," Bednarik said, "you can get up now. The game is over."

After the game, Shaw praised Bednarik for playing 58 of the game's 60 minutes. The 35-year-old Bednarik—by far the oldest player on the field—had held the team together on offense and defense.

"It amazes me when I think about it," Bednarik said after the game. "But then, it was mind over matter. We were winning, and that's what was important."

Bednarik's performance marked the end of an NFL era. He was the last man to play both offense and defense for an entire NFL game. A few years later, Bednarik was named the best center in the first 50 years of professional football.

Vermeil

In 1961, quarterback Sonny Jurgenson led the Eagles to second place in the Eastern Division. But then Philadelphia turned into perennial losers, and Jurgenson was traded to the Washington Redskins.

In 1966, the Eagles temporarily broke their losing habit by finishing second in the division, but that was their best season until the late 1970s.

Throughout that long losing streak, the Eagles did everything they could to turn the team around. They changed coaches and quarterbacks. They even changed the color of their helmets. Nothing seemed to work. Though they had their share of star players—like wide receiver Harold Carmichael, center Guy Morriss, tackles Jerry Sisemore and Stan Walters, and safety Randy Logan—none of the Eagles knew what it was like to play for a winning team.

That all changed in 1976—the year Dick Vermeil became head coach. Vermeil had been a successful college coach at UCLA. In 1975, he led his team to a Rose Bowl victory over Ohio State.

When he joined the Eagles, Vermeil called a press conference and predicted confidently that, in five years, the Eagles would be Super Bowl material.

The critics doubted Vermeil. After all, the Eagles had only one winning season in the last 15 years. But Vermeil knew he could rebuild the Eagles into champions. Vermeil worked as hard as any coach in the NFL. He did not go home at night, choosing instead to sleep for a few hours on his office cot.

The Eagles had talent. But the players needed a winning attitude. To build that winning spirit, Philadelphia needed a team leader on the field. That leader was quarterback Ron Jaworski.

"Jaws"

In 1977, Jaworski came to the Eagles from the Los Angeles Rams. "Jaws" was known as a quarterback who did not accept losing. But when he first got to Philadelphia, he found the team shell-shocked from losing. They were quiet and kept to themselves. They had been through some lean years, and they didn't know what it was like to have fun playing football.

Jaworski knew that attitude had to change. He went around patting guys on the back, telling them everything was going to be all right. It was time for the Eagles to become winners.

Coach Dick Vermeil was hired to lead the Eagles in 1976.

Jaworski's new teammates didn't know what to make of him. Some thought he was crazy. Every other quarterback they had known had been a loner or very businesslike. Jaworski wasn't like that. He often laughed and yelled and told the team they were going to be winners. Philadelphia was coming off a 4-10 record, and he was talking about winning a title.

But Jaworski knew exactly what he was saying. He spent long hours with Vermeil, studying films and devising ways the Eagles could use Jaworski's rifle arm. All the hard work paid off as the Eagles played better and better.

In 1978, the Eagles put together their best season in years. Running back Wilbert Montgomery gave the Eagles their best rushing threat in the entire decade. With the ground game in high gear, Jaworski passed more efficiently. Carmichael gained the most yardage of any NFC receiver and ran his pass catching string to 96 games.

The Eagles were in the playoff hunt all season. But then they lost two straight and were 8-7 going into the final game. They needed a win to record their first winning season since 1966 and earn a spot in the playoffs.

After Vermeil gave an inspiring pregame speech, the Eagles charged out of the locker room and whipped the New York Giants 20-3. After the game, Jaworski returned to the locker room and screamed, "We're winners! We're winners!" Jaworski then saw Eagles owner Leonard Tose. "Hey, boss, we're winners!" Jaworski shouted as he gave Tose a hug.

Tose turned to Vermeil and congratulated him. "I couldn't have done it without you," Vermeil said as he buried his head on Tose's shoulder. Together, the owner and coach cried like babies. The Eagles were finally winners—and in the playoffs for the first time since 1960. Unfortunately for Eagles fans, Atlanta ended Philadelphia's season with a 14-13 comeback win in the first round.

The following season, Philadelphia returned to the playoffs with an impressive 11-5 record. This time, they defeated the Chicago Bears 27-17 in the first round. In the second round, they traveled to Tampa Bay to play the Buccaneers. Tampa jumped out to a 17-7 halftime lead and never looked back. A fourth-quarter Harold Carmichael touchdown made the score respectable, but the Eagles lost 24-17. The Super Bowl would have to wait another year—but only one.

Ron Jaworski came to the Eagles from the Los Angeles Rams in 1977.

A Super Season

In 1980, Philadelphia soared to an 11-1 record in late November as the offense and defense played brilliantly. But with a playoff berth already locked up, the Eagles went into a skid.

Going into the final game against Dallas, the Eagles held a one-game lead over the Cowboys. To win first place, Dallas needed to beat the Eagles by 25 points or more. It seemed unlikely that Philadelphia would give up so many points, especially since their defense was playing so well. But early in the fourth quarter, Dallas seized a 35-10 lead and threatened to add more.

That's when Jaworski and his teammates finally took charge of the game. In a furious comeback, the Eagles scored 17 fourth-quarter points for a 35-27 final score in favor of Dallas. Though both teams had identical 12-4 records, Philadelphia won the division title by scoring more points throughout the season than Dallas. It was the Eagles' first division crown since 1960.

Bergey, Charles Johnson, Carl Hairston, Randy Logan and Jerry Robinson were the defensive stars. On offense, Jaworski, Montgomery, Carmichael and wide receiver Charlie Smith had outstanding seasons.

In the playoffs, the Eagles had little trouble with Minnesota, defeating the Vikings 31-16. But now, in the NFC Championship game, they would have to face their rivals, the Dallas Cowboys, to earn a trip to the Super Bowl.

The two teams played to a 7-7 halftime tie. But in the third quarter, the Eagles took advantage of Dallas mistakes and tacked on 10 points for a 17-7 lead. The defense took over from there and held the Cowboys scoreless. Philadelphia added another field goal for a 20-7 win. In the game, Montgomery ran for 194 yards—2 yards shy of the playoff record set by Steve Van Buren in 1947. More importantly, the Eagles were going to the Super Bowl for the first time in their long history. Coach Vermeil had lived up to his promise.

But in Super Bowl XV in New Orleans, the Eagles ran into a tough Oakland Raiders team. Oakland seized a 14-3 halftime lead, then added 10 more third-quarter points for an insurmountable 24-3 advantage. The Eagles' lone touchdown came in the fourth quarter. The Raiders won easily, 27-10.

But Jaworski was proud of his team after the game. They were no longer doormats. They were Super Bowl material. Eventually, Jaworski was named the NFL Player of the Year for leading the Eagles to the Super Bowl.

Despite the Super Bowl loss, Philadelphia's future looked bright. The Eagles still had the talent for a Super Bowl return. In 1981, they jumped out to a 7-1 record. But then the Eagles went into a tailspin and finished with a 10-6 record. Still, they had defeated the Cardinals 38-0 in the final game to make the playoffs. And it looked as though the Eagles were returning to Super Bowl form just in time. But in the playoffs, Philadelphia lost 27-21 at home to the New York Giants.

In 1982, Vermeil returned one more year for another stab at the Super Bowl. This time, however, the Eagles fell victim to the players strike as they lost their first four games once the walkout had ended. Stating he was "burned out," Vermeil retired after the season, leaving the team in disarray.

To return to championship form, the Eagles needed to rebuild the team around a strong defensive player. In 1985, that player joined the team. He would become the Eagles' most dominant defensive player since Chuck Bednarik.

PHILADELPHIA EAGLES

Coach Dick Vermeil is hired to lead the Eagles in 1976.

Chuck Bednarik signs with the Eagles in 1949.

Norm Van Brocklin plays quarterback in the 1950s and 1960s.

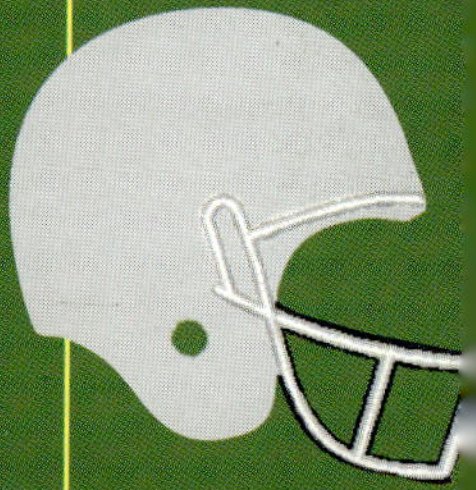

Ron Jaworski comes to the Eagles from the Los Angeles Rams in 1977.

In 1993, Bubby Brister sets the club record for fewest interceptions in a season.

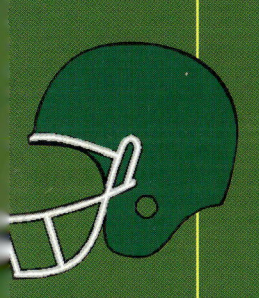

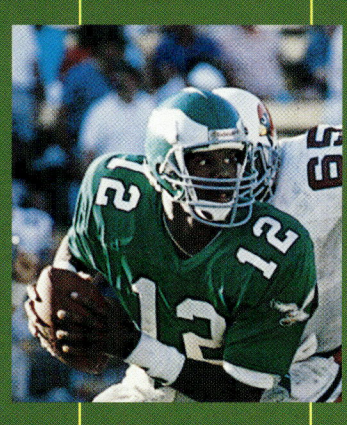

The Eagles take Randall Cunningham in the second round of the 1985 draft.

PHILADELPHIA EAGLES

The Minister of Defense

Defensive end Reggie White already had professional football experience when he came to the Eagles. White had played two years with the Memphis Showboats in the United States Football League (USFL). During his career with Memphis, teammates called White the "Minister of Defense" not only because he was a Baptist minister, but because White was the most dominant defensive player in the USFL.

When White was a child, he was always bigger than the other children. They often teased him about his size, calling him "Bigfoot" or "Land of the Giant." Once in seventh grade, White discovered he was good at playing football—and that he could use his size and achieve success by playing within the rules. He even recalled telling his mother that someday he would be a professional football player, and that he would take care of her the rest of her life. It was a promise he would keep.

White was a multi-talented football player. He could rush the passer and also stop the run—something he was especially proud of. "The so-called men of the game pride themselves on being complete players," White said. "Sacks are great, and they get you elected to the Pro Bowl. But I've always felt that a great defensive lineman has to play the run and the pass equally well."

Offensive linemen had great difficulty blocking White. Though he was big and strong, he was also very quick and fast. "He can kill you with his speed," said San Francisco tackle Harris Barton. "But if you overplay it and open up too wide, he'll rush inside, and you're finished. The first thing you have to worry about is his power. If he gets his hands on you, then he's like an offensive lineman. He'll drive you right into the backfield."

Reggie White (92) tosses his helmet after receiving a penalty for roughing the passer.

    White was with the Eagles for two years when the team hired Buddy Ryan as their head coach. White and his defensive teammates were pleased with the selection because Ryan, as the defensive coach of the 1985 Chicago Bears, helped his team win the Super Bowl with one of the best defensive squads since Pittsburgh's famed "Steel Curtain." The Eagles hoped Ryan could help the Eagles build another powerful defense that would propel them to the Super Bowl.

    When Ryan joined the team, the Eagles were young and needed leadership. White was their star, but Philadelphia needed more talent at other key positions—especially at quarterback. Ryan already had his eye on such a player. His name was Randall Cunningham.

Randall

Randall Cunningham had all the tools to become a great NFL quarterback. He was tall, strong, fast, and had a rifle arm. But he was also inexperienced, and Ryan would have to be patient with his young quarterback as he developed his skills.

When Cunningham was young, he dreamed of playing professional football. His older brother, Sam, had been a star fullback at the University of Southern California (USC). Sam Cunningham also starred for several years with the New England Patriots until injuries cut his career short.

Randall Cunningham eventually played college football at the University of Nevada-Las Vegas where he struggled to establish himself. But his arm strength and throwing ability was too hard for the coaches to ignore, and slowly Cunningham received more and more playing time.

Eventually, Cunningham became a star at UNLV. But both his parents died during his sophomore year. Their deaths made Cunningham more determined than ever to become a successful professional football player.

The Eagles chose Cunningham in the second round of the 1985 college draft. He didn't see much action his rookie year. But when Ryan joined the team, the new head coach decided that Cunningham was going to be his quarterback.

Ryan's faith in his young quarterback paid off in 1987. That year, Cunningham threw 23 touchdown passes—the third most in the National Football Conference (NFC). He also led the team in rushing with 505 yards.

But Cunningham wasn't the only success story that year. Reggie White had 21 sacks—tops in the NFL. Wide receiver Mike Quick caught 11 touchdown passes, the second most in the NFL. Though the rest of the defense was disappointing, the Eagles were slowly building a playoff contender.

The Eagles took Randall Cunningham in the second round of the 1985 draft.

Division Champs

In 1988, everything came together for Ryan's Philadelphia Eagles as they won the NFC Eastern Division title with a 10-6 record. Cunningham threw for 3,808 yards and led the team in rushing for the second straight year. Even more, he was named to the Pro Bowl team, as was White, who led the league in sacks with 18. Rookie tight end Keith Jackson also earned All-Pro honors by catching 81 passes. Running back Keith Byars scored 10 touchdowns and was one of the league's top receivers with 72 catches. However, wide receiver Mike Quick broke his leg and missed half the season.

In the playoffs, Philadelphia traveled to Chicago to face the Bears—Ryan's former team. In a game dubbed "The Fog Bowl" because of the fog that enveloped Soldier Field, the Eagles fell behind 17-9 at halftime. All Philadelphia could manage after that was a third-quarter field goal. The season ended with a 20-12 loss. The Eagles would have to work harder if they wanted to make the Super Bowl.

In 1989, the Eagles remained in first place for much of the season. But then the wheels starting coming off. Though he led the team in rushing for the third straight year, Cunningham had trouble moving the offense. Even worse, assistant coach Doug Scovil died of a heart attack after a practice.

The defense showed improvement. Defensive linemen Clyde Simmons and Jerome Brown combined for 26 sacks. Reggie White

Cunningham led the Eagles to the division title in 1988.

made the Pro Bowl again, and Eric Allen led the NFC with eight interceptions.

Although they didn't win their division, the Eagles' 11-5 record earned them a wildcard berth in the playoffs. Playing at home against the Los Angeles Rams, Philadelphia fell behind 14-0 in the first quarter and couldn't catch up. The disappointing 21-7 loss ended their season, but hopes remained high.

In 1990, the Eagles bounced back from a 1-3 start to make the playoffs for the third straight year. Cunningham remained the NFL's top offensive threat. He just missed becoming the first quarterback to run and pass for over 1,000 yards each. Although he led the Eagles in rushing for the fourth straight season, he got help from his running backs, particularly Heath Sherman. Ryan was fired after the season for the team's failure to win their first-round playoff game at home against the Washington Redskins, who beat them 20-6.

Quarterback Jim McMahon scrambles away from defenseman Michael Dean Perry of the Cleveland Browns.

The following season, disaster struck. New head coach Rich Kotite knew his team's chances to make the playoffs were shattered when Cunningham suffered a season-ending knee injury only 18 minutes into the first game. Backup Jim McMahon battled many injuries and rallied the Eagles back into playoff contention. But when McMahon was not in the lineup, the Eagles were forced to start veteran Pat Ryan and rookie Brad Goebel through a four-game losing streak.

The big story was the defense. The Eagles led the league in fewest total yards, fewest rushing yards and fewest passing yards—only the fifth team ever to achieve that rare triple. However, their 10-6 record did not get them into the playoffs.

In 1992, the Eagles suffered more bad news. Jerome Brown was killed in a car accident before training camp began. Keith Jackson held out and signed with the Miami Dolphins. By the end of the year, Reggie White, Seth Joyner, and Clyde Simmons said they were leaving the team to play elsewhere.

But Cunningham returned to the lineup and threw 19 touchdown passes. The Eagles also had acquired Herschel Walker in a June trade, and he responded with over 1,000 yards rushing and 10 touchdowns. The defense was again the league's best. The Eagles finished with an 11-5 record—good enough for second place in the Eastern division and a playoff berth.

In the first round against the New Orleans Saints, the Eagles fell behind 17-7 at the half and trailed 20-10 heading into the fourth quarter. Then the Eagles' offense exploded. Cunningham threw a 35-yard touchdown pass to Fred Barnett. Sherman followed that with a 6-yard touchdown run. Reggie White sacked Saints' quarterback Bobby Hebert (pronounced HAY-bear) in the end zone for a 2-point safety. Then Roger Ruzek tacked on a 39-yard field goal. Eric Allen finished the scoring with an 18-yard touchdown interception return, making the final score 36-20 in favor of Philadelphia. Now it was on to Dallas to face the Cowboys.

The game started out like the previous one. The Eagles fell behind 17-3 at halftime. But the Cowboys had a better defense than the Saints and shut down Cunningham. The Eagles lost 34-10, ending their season with huge question marks about their team—especially the defense.

Surprise Starts

Despite the player losses, the Eagles surprised everyone when they won their first four games of the 1993 season and took the lead in the NFC East. Then disaster struck as Cunningham suffered a broken leg. The Eagles then lost six straight games with Ken O'Brien and Bubby Brister at quarterback. Injuries also knocked out Barnett, linebacker Tim Harris, and several other veterans.

Brister finally came around late in the season. He set a team record for fewest interceptions and ranked fourth in the conference in passing. The Eagles won their final three games to finish with an 8-8 record. But they did not make the playoffs. The one bright spot was Eric Allen. He tied an NFL record when he returned four of his six interceptions for touchdowns.

It was hard to be too optimistic in 1994 about the Eagles' Super Bowl chances. No major trades occurred and no new stars were emerging. The Eagles lost their opener 28-23 to the New York Giants. But then they strung four wins in a row to tie Dallas for first place after Week 6. After a loss in Week 7, the Eagles won three more—including a Week 10 victory over Buddy Ryan's Phoenix Cardinals. With the victory, the Eagles moved to 7-2, just one game behind the Cowboys. It was their best start since 1981.

In 1993, Bubby Brister set a team record for fewest interceptions and was ranked fourth in the conference in passing.

The wheels began to come off the following week. The Cleveland Browns rolled over the Eagles 26-7. The next game was the rematch against Ryan and the Cardinals in Phoenix. The Eagles lost 12-6. In Week 13, Philadelphia lost to Atlanta 28-21. Suddenly, their record had slipped to 7-5. They were still in second place. But they trailed the Cowboys by three games. Even worse, their playoff chances were now in jeopardy.

Philadelphia could not stop the bleeding. They lost their final four games to fall to 7-9 and out of the playoffs. The final loss in Cincinnati was a bitter pill to swallow. Bengals' placekicker Doug Pelfrey kicked two field goals in the last three seconds to beat the Eagles 33-30. Pelfrey's first field goal tied the score 30-30 with three seconds left. The Bengals got the ball back when cornerback Adrian Hardy recovered a fumble on the next kickoff on the Eagles' 35 with one second left. Pelfrey then kicked a wobbly 54-yard field goal to win the game.

After starting the season 7-2, the Eagles had lost their last seven games. Kotite was fired two days later.

§

The Eagles remain a team in transition. They still have the services of star quarterback Randall Cunningham. But gone are the days of a dominating defense. It will take the Eagles many years of sound draft choices and trades if they are to regain their status as one of the NFL's best teams. If Cunningham can stay healthy, the Eagles may get there.

GLOSSARY

ALL-PRO—A player who is voted to the Pro Bowl.
BACKFIELD—Players whose position is behind the line of scrimmage.
CORNERBACK—Either of two defensive halfbacks stationed a short distance behind the linebackers and relatively near the sidelines.
DEFENSIVE END—A defensive player who plays on the end of the line and often next to the defensive tackle.
DEFENSIVE TACKLE—A defensive player who plays on the line and between the guard and end.
ELIGIBLE—A player who is qualified to be voted into the Hall of Fame.
END ZONE—The area on either end of a football field where players score touchdowns.
EXTRA POINT—The additional one-point score added after a player makes a touchdown. Teams earn extra points if the placekicker kicks the ball through the uprights of the goalpost, or if an offensive player crosses the goal line with the football before being tackled.
FIELD GOAL—A three-point score awarded when a placekicker kicks the ball through the uprights of the goalpost.
FULLBACK—An offensive player who often lines up farthest behind the front line.
FUMBLE—When a player loses control of the football.
GUARD—An offensive lineman who plays between the tackles and center.
GROUND GAME—The running game.
HALFBACK—An offensive player whose position is behind the line of scrimmage.
HALFTIME—The time period between the second and third quarters of a football game.
INTERCEPTION—When a defensive player catches a pass from an offensive player.
KICK RETURNER—An offensive player who returns kickoffs.
LINEBACKER—A defensive player whose position is behind the line of scrimmage.
LINEMAN—An offensive or defensive player who plays on the line of scrimmage.
PASS—To throw the ball.
PASS RECEIVER—An offensive player who runs pass routes and catches passes.
PLACEKICKER—An offensive player who kicks extra points and field goals. The placekicker also kicks the ball from a tee to the opponent after his team has scored.

PLAYOFFS—The postseason games played amongst the division winners and wild card teams which determines the Super Bowl champion.
PRO BOWL—The postseason All-Star game which showcases the NFL's best players.
PUNT—To kick the ball to the opponent.
QUARTER—One of four 15-minute time periods that makes up a football game.
QUARTERBACK—The backfield player who usually calls the signals for the plays.
REGULAR SEASON—The games played after the preseason and before the playoffs.
ROOKIE—A first-year player.
RUNNING BACK—A backfield player who usually runs with the ball.
RUSH—To run with the football.
SACK—To tackle the quarterback behind the line of scrimmage.
SAFETY—A defensive back who plays behind the linemen and linebackers. Also, two points awarded for tackling an offensive player in his own end zone when he's carrying the ball.
SPECIAL TEAMS—Squads of football players that perform special tasks (for example, kickoff team and punt-return team).
SPONSOR—A person or company that finances a football team.
SUPER BOWL—The NFL championship game played between the AFC champion and the NFC champion.
T FORMATION—An offensive formation in which the fullback lines up behind the center and quarterback with one halfback stationed on each side of the fullback.
TACKLE—An offensive or defensive lineman who plays between the ends and the guards.
TAILBACK—The offensive back farthest from the line of scrimmage.
TIGHT END—An offensive lineman who is stationed next to the tackles, and who usually blocks or catches passes.
TOUCHDOWN—When one team crosses the goal line of the other team's end zone. A touchdown is worth six points.
TURNOVER—To turn the ball over to an opponent either by a fumble, an interception, or on downs.
UNDERDOG—The team that is picked to lose the game.
WIDE RECEIVER—An offensive player who is stationed relatively close to the sidelines and who usually catches passes.
WILD CARD—A team that makes the playoffs without winning its division.
ZONE PASS DEFENSE—A pass defense method where defensive backs defend a certain area of the playing field rather than individual pass receivers.

INDEX

A

Allen, Eric 25-27

B

Barnett, Fred 26, 27
Barton, Harris 20
Bednarik, Chuck 4, 7, 9, 10, 11, 17
Bell, Bert 6
Brister, Bubby 27
Brookshier, Tom 10
Brown, Jerome 4, 24, 26
Byars, Keith 24

C

Carmichael, Harold 4, 12, 14, 15, 16
Chicago Bears 21
Cleveland Browns 28
Cunningham, Randall 4, 21, 22-28
Cunningham, Sam 22

E

Eastern Division 6, 7, 10, 12, 24, 26

F

Frankfort Yellow Jackets 6
Franklin Field 10, 11

G

Goebel, Brad 25

H

Hairston, Carl 16
Hebert, Bobby 26

J

Jackson, Keith 24, 26
Jaworski, Ron 4, 12-14, 16, 17
Johnson, Charles 16
Joyner, Seth 26
Jurgenson, Sonny 4, 12

K

Kotite, Rich 25, 28

L

Logan, Randy 12, 16
Lombardi, Vince 10
Los Angeles Rams 9, 13, 25
Louisiana State University 7

M

McMahon, Jim 25
Memphis Showboats 20
Miami Dolphins 26
Montgomery, Wilbert 4, 14, 16
Morriss, Guy 12

N

National Football Conference 23
Neale, Earl "Greasy" 6
New England Patriots 22
New Orleans Saints 26
New York Giants 14, 27
NFL championship 4

31

O

Oakland Raiders 4, 17
O'Brien, Davey 6
O'Brien, Ken 27

P

Pelfrey, Doug 28
Phoenix Cardinals 27
Pihos, Pete 7
Player of the Year 17
playoffs 14, 15, 25-28
Pro Bowl 20, 24

Q

Quick, Mike 23, 24

R

Robinson, Jerry 16
Rose Bowl 12
Ruzek, Roger 26
Ryan, Buddy 21-25, 27, 28
Ryan, Pat 25

S

Scovil, Doug 24
Sherman, Heath 25, 26
Simmons, Clyde 4, 24, 26
Sisemore, Jerry 12
Smith, Charlie 16
Starr, Bart 10, 11
Super Bowl 4, 17

T

Taylor, Jim 11
Thompson, Alexis 6
Thompson, Tommy 7
Tose, Leonard 14

U

UCLA 12
University of Southern California 22
UNLV 22
USFL 20

V

Van Brocklin, Norm 4, 9, 10
Van Buren, Steve 7, 17
Vermeil, Dick 12, 14, 17

W

Walker, Herschel 26
Walters, Stan 12
Washington Redskins 12, 25
White, Reggie 4, 20, 21, 23, 24, 26
Wray, Lud 6

796.332 $18.00
Ita   Italia, Bob
           The Philadel-
         phia Eagles.

DATE DUE

SEP 16 2002	DEC 19 2003		
OCT 30 2003	NOV 04 2004		
NOV 08 2003	NOV 29 2004		
JAN 02 2005	FEB 01		
JAN 14 2003	MAR 14 2005		
JAN 29 2003	APR 11 2005		
FEB 05 2003	MAY 09	NOV 14 2005	
MAR 10 2003			
JAN 15 2004			
	NOV 15		
JAN 23 2004	NOV 22 2005		
JAN 29 2004	OCT 24 2006		
MAR 04 2004	APR 12 2007		
JAN 04	NOV 11 2008		
MAR 14 2004	FEB 03 2009		
SEP 2	SEP 2		

St. Odilia School Library
3495 North Victoria
Shoreview, MN 55126